Half Acre

Sarah Frankel

LifeRich Publishing is a registered trademark of The Reader's Digest Association, Inc.

LifeRich Publishing books may be ordered through booksellers or by contacting:

LifeRich Publishing
1663 Liberty Drive
Bloomington, IN 47403
www.liferichpublishing.com
1 (888) 238-8637

ISBN: 978-1-4897-1397-1 (sc)
ISBN: 978-1-4897-1396-4 (e)

Print information available on the last page.

LifeRich Publishing rev. date: 9/28/2017

Half Acre

Especially for my little
outdoor explorers.

My yard is half an acre;
most would consider it small,
but a wild tangle of nature,
lives here winter, spring,
summer and fall.

Thrushes are found
everywhere,
warbling sweet notes
from the trees,
and woven with
mosses and hair,
vireo nests sway along
in the breeze.

Below on the woodland floor,
ribbons of light dance around.
Here, trout lilies are the décor;
orchids and trillium
paint the ground.

The milkweed patch is alive
with the zig-zagging
travel of bees,
and as pollen is brought
to the hive,
swallowtails sail in
on the breeze.

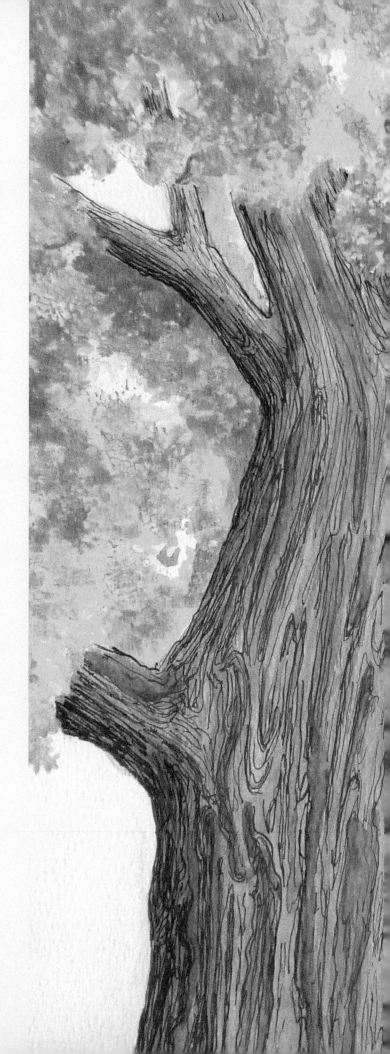

Mighty red oaks are strapping
in their green cloaks
high above.
Broad leaves are
lazily flapping,
stretching up to the
sun they so love.

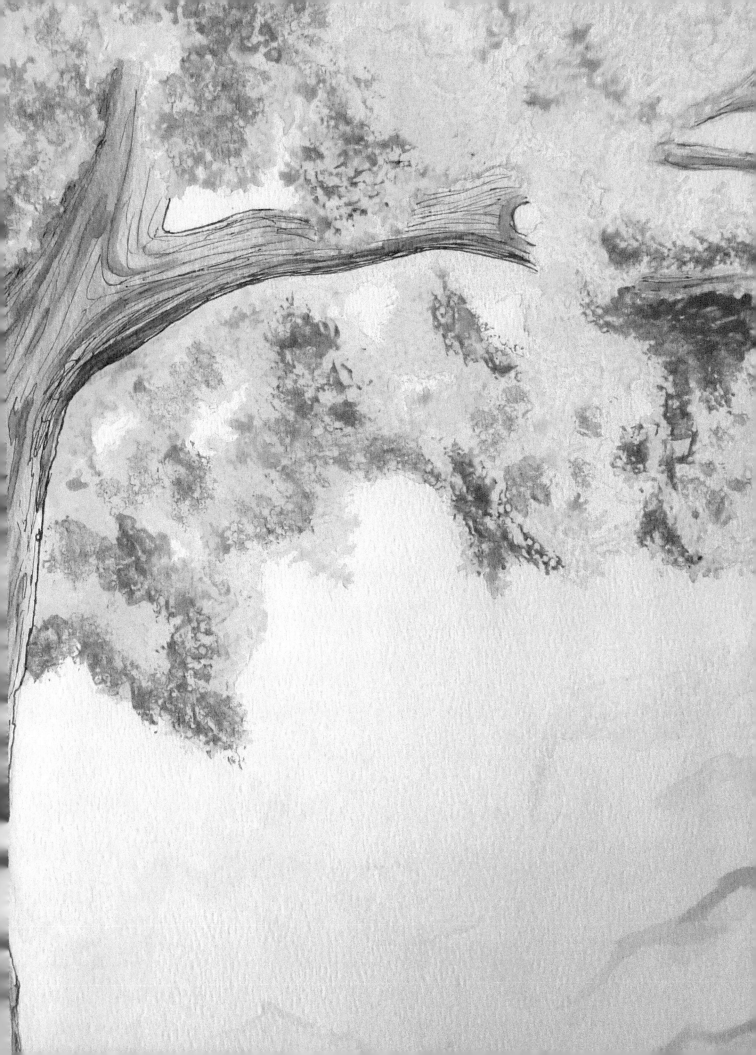

An old stump slowly
breaks down,
draped with moss
and ferns galore.
White-lipped snails glide
on the damp ground,
decomposing the
dark forest floor.

At dusk, the North
Star appears,
and in the quarter moon's light,
a chorus of sounds
you might hear,
as red foxes yip into the night.

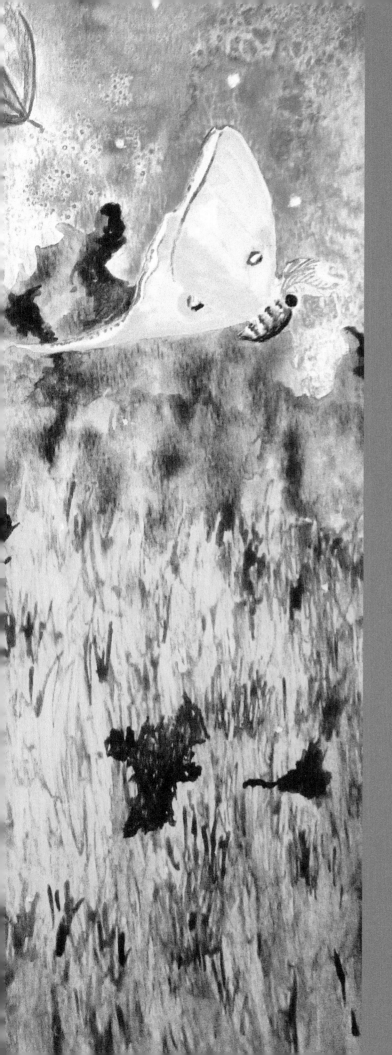

A luna moth flutters past,
while bats follow closely behind.
A barred owl's shadow is cast
on a hare that has
run out of time.

The sky is a highway for clouds,
rolling past at rapid speeds.
Nighthawks swoop and
dive in large crowds,
flying south eating
gnats as they please.

The land is splashed
with colors:
maples orange, yellow and red.
Asters bloom later than others;
Autumn weaving her
lavender thread.

During the cold of winter,
tunneling through lacey snow,
mice, voles and other
small leapers
avoid hunters above and below.

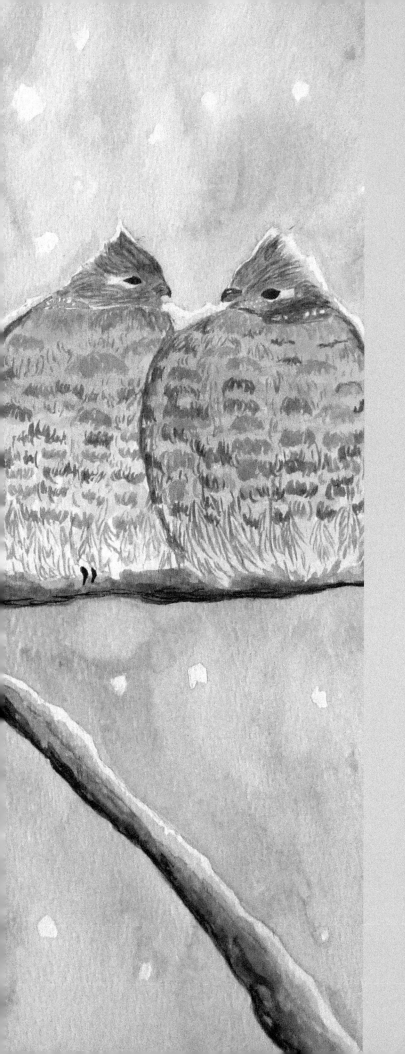

For warmth, grouse
roost together,
while squirrels nap
nestled in straw.
Tree frogs await
warmer weather,
when their bodies will
eventually thaw.

Chickadees sing "Hey Sweetie"!
Their song is heard far and near.
Chipmunks emerge
still quite sleepy,
relieved that spring
is finally here!

Maybe your yard's
small like mine,
maybe it stretches for miles,
maybe there's swaying
white pines
or a small patch of dirt
and wood piles.

But...
whether your yard's
large or small,
Nature will open her wings.
Step outside and discover it all,
beyond your door
awaits wild things.

Author Biography

Sarah Frankel is a mother, naturalist and a child at heart. She lives in Conway, NH where she teaches science at the local middle school. Her lifelong goal is to help children build stronger relationships with the natural world around them.